HÄGAR®

TH...

Haga...

DIK BROWNE

ATTICA
PUBLICATIONS

Introducing . . .

HÄGAR THE HORRIBLE a hard-working Barbarian businessman. He's in sacking and looting.

His wife, HELGA. She finds civilising Hägar a 24-hour-a-day job!

This is HAMLET, their son, a real problem child! He insists on wearing his hair short, bathing, reading and otherwise behaving in a very unbarbarian manner.

HONI, their daughter, is sixteen years old, and still not married!

But that's not the end of Hägars troubles . . . there's also LUCKY EDDIE who must be the most hopeless assistant in history!

First published by Attica Publications 1986

Attica Publications, an imprint of Argus Communications Ltd., DLM House, Edinburgh Way, Harlow, Essex CM20 2HL, England.

ISBN 1 85176 026 1

Printed and bound in Great Britain by Cox & Wyman Ltd, Reading

!!☆◎#!! MISSED!
!!. MISSED AGAIN! AND AGAIN!
IT'S HOPELESS
IS SPLIT-PEA SOUP THE *ONLY* SOUP YOU LIKE?
BROWNE

IF WE DON'T KEEP FIGHTING THEY'LL BREAK IN AND TAKE EVERYTHING WE OWN!
RIGHT! YOU TELL THEM WE'LL NEVER GIVE UP!!

YOU TELL THEM! THEY'RE YOUR RELATIVES!
DIK BROWNE

WHEN YOU GROW UP YOU'LL FIND THAT PEOPLE ARE PRETTY MUCH THE SAME THE WHOLE WORLD OVER
DIK BROWNE

GEE, DAD, THAT'S A NICE THOUGHT
YEAH...

THAT'S WHY I GOT THIS NICE SHIELD

I'M HOME FROM PARIS, HELGA !
OH, GOOD! DID YOU BRING ME SOME DIFFERENT-SHAPED COOKIE CUTTERS ?

YES !

EVERY VIKING SHOULD HAVE A GOAL... DO YOU HAVE A GOAL, LUCKY EDDIE ?

I SAID: DO YOU HAVE A GOAL?!

I'M LOOKING! I'M LOOKING!!
DIK BROWNE

SOME BRAVE MAN MUST FIND THE WAY THROUGH THE DANGEROUS PASS OF DOOM — WHAT SAY YOU?
DIK BROWNE

AH!
MAY I BE EXCUSED?

PARDON ME, STRANGER... WHERE ARE WE ?
THIS IS THE ROAD TO TOMORROW AND THIS IS A PLACE CALLED TODAY IT'S A WONDERFUL PLACE TO VISIT BUT NO ONE MAY EVER STAY
NEVER ASK FOR DIRECTIONS IN IRELAND !

WHAT A DOPE!
I TOLD YOU TO DIG A HOLE BIG ENOUGH FOR THREE MEN!

BUT I DID
YES, HE DID
YES
DIK BROWNE

WHAT DO YOU WANT FOR YOUR BIRTHDAY, BABY?
ALL I WANT IS YOUR HAPPINESS
AWWW... I AM HAPPY, DARLING!
HOW CAN YOU BE HAPPY WHEN YOUR WIFE HAS NEVER HAD A DIAMOND?
DIK BROWNE

ARE THOSE YOUR RED SOCKS ?!
YEAH... I'M DRYING THEM

GET THEM OUT! THEY MAKE THE SHIP LOOK TERRIBLE!
DIK BROWNE

HERE COMES THE ENEMY AND WE'RE OUTNUMBERED! LET'S HIDE BEHIND THOSE TWO TREES!
OKAY

MIND IF I MAKE A SUGGESTION?
DIK BROWNE

REMEMBER, DEAR, BE SHY! MEN FEEL THREATENED BY STRONG WOMEN!
WHY IS THAT?
BECAUSE MEN ARE NINNIES!
DIK BROWNE

ARE YOU GOING TO TAKE OUT THIS GARBAGE?
WHEN I'M READY! PUT IT DOWN!

DIK BROWNE
WE GO THROUGH THIS EVERY DAY!

EVER NOTICE HOW I START TO SAY SOMETHING AND ...
I FINISH THE SENTENCE ?

I GUESS IT HAPPENS TO PEOPLE WHO'VE...
BEEN MARRIED A LONG TIME ?

YEAH, IT'S A REAL PAIN IN THE ...
BROWNE

WE REALLY SHOULD DO SOMETHING ABOUT HIS FLEAS

I'M AFRAID IF WE DON'T, THEY'LL GET ON THE DOG...
DIK BROWNE

WHERE'S DADDY ?
I MADE HIM EAT OUTSIDE BECAUSE HE'S BEEN FIGHTING
BUT HE'S **ALWAYS** FIGHTING!
NOT WITH A SKUNK
DIK BROWNE

HI, HELGA...
I'M HOME!
GOOD. YOU JUST HAVE TIME TO FRESHEN UP BEFORE DINNER

WHAT ARE YOU DOING?!
I'M FRESHENING UP
DIK BROWNE
XXX

WHAT DO YOU WANT TO DO TODAY?
I DUNNO...

PART OF ME WANTS TO GO SWIMMING AND PART OF ME WANTS TO GET TAN
UNDERSTANDABLE
DIK BROWNE

HAGAR NEVER STRIKES THE FIRST BLOW

HE IS A WISE MAN
YES... AND A GREAT COUNTERPUNCHER!
DIK BROWNE

LOOK AT THOSE STARS! DON'T THEY MAKE YOU FEEL SMALL AND INSIGNIFICANT AND UNIMPORTANT ?
YEAH...
DIK BROWNE

STARS!

YOU SHOULDN'T ARGUE!
THIS ISN'T AN ARGUMENT... IT'S A DISCUSSION
YOUR MOTHER THINKS HER MOTHER SHOULD SPEND PART OF THE WINTER WITH US AND AND I DON'T.
DIK BROWNE
THE WHOLE WINTER
OH, WELL... NOW IT'S AN ARGUMENT!

SO WHAT DO YOU THINK OF HERNIA ?
SHE KNOCKS ME OUT

YOU HEAR THAT ? I THINK HAMLET'S IN LOVE!
DIK BROWNE

HEY! WATCH WHERE YOU'RE SHOOTING THAT THING!
ZING
DIK BROWNE

@!!☆!
YOU HIT A
A CLOUD!

I PUT MY UNDERWEAR ON INSIDE OUT
THAT'S SUPPOSED TO BE LUCKY! WHEN DID YOU DO IT?

SIX YEARS AGO
DIK BROWNE

I WONDER IF HAGAR HAS A HANGOVER?
QUIET!
IS THAT A YES?
DIK BROWNE

SON—IN THIS WORLD YOU HAVE TO MAKE YOUR OWN BREAKS...
DIK BROWNE
A NICE BIG CLUB WILL HELP

DID THOSE GUYS LOOK FAMILIAR TO YOU ?

NAW
ISSja KIKKUM BOBOS CON NOO ?
NAJ!
DIK BROWNE

HELP!.....
I'M BEING HELD PRISONER BY AN EVIL WIZARD!
I THOUGHT MAIDENS WERE ALWAYS HELD PRISONER IN A TALL TOWER
DIK BROWNE
I'M AFRAID OF HEIGHTS

THERE ARE SEVEN AGES OF MAN...
THREE

FIRST: 'I WANT IT!'
THEN: 'I GOT IT!'
AND FINALLY: 'YOU'VE HAD IT...'
DIK BROWNE

YOU'RE NEVER SATISFIED!
YOU WANT TO EAT YOUR CAKE AND STILL HAVE IT
YEAH....
DIK BROWNE

LISTEN GOOD! I'M GOING TO SAY THIS ONCE, AND ONE TIME ONLY, AND I'M NOT GOING TO REPEAT IT!!

THINK! THINK! THINK!
? ?
DIK BROWNE

HELGA! GUESS WHO WAS CROWNED QUEEN OF THE MAY
DIK BROWNE

GUESS!

AW, COME ON–GUESS!

TAKE YOUR FEET OFF THAT TABLE!
OKAY...

AND DON'T TILT YOUR CHAIR!
NEVER SATISFIED!
DIK BROWNE

BOY! THIS GUY IS TRICKY!!
YOU NEVER HAD THIS MUCH TROUBLE BEFORE

I NEVER FOUGHT A SPANIARD BEFORE!
DIK BROWNE

PSST! ARE THE ENEMY BORDER GUARDS GONE?
YES, HAGAR
DIK BROWNE

OW!

SURRENDER OR ELSE!!
TAKE YOUR HAT OFF WHEN YOU TALK TO A LADY!!
WACK!
YOU'RE NO LADY, MACBETH !!

I HATE THIS RUG YOU GOT IN BAGDAD!
WHAT'S WRONG WITH IT?

I CAN'T GET IT TO LIE FLAT
DIK BROWNE

DID YOU GIVE LUCKY EDDIE A ROPE AND TELL HIM TO WALK THE DOG?
YEAH

...WHY DO YOU ASK?
DIK BROWNE

WHAT KIND OF FISH ARE THOSE?
DIK BROWNE

FLYING FISH

HOLD IT, DADDY!
IT'S IMPOLITE TO START EATING
UNTIL MAMA SITS DOWN, TOO!

DIK BROWNE

THERE GOES IVOR... EVERYTHING HE CAN BEG, BORROW OR STEAL GOES ON HIS WIFE'S BACK!
SHE MUST BE A TERRIBLE WIFE!
NOT REALLY...
DIK BROWNE

SOON WE SAIL FOR ENGLAND!
WHAT ARE WE WAITING FOR?

HIGH TIDE
DIK BROWNE

GEE, THIS IS AN AWFULLY FANCY RESTAURANT. CAN WE AFFORD IT ?
DON'T WORRY. WE'RE ONLY HERE FOR THE BRUNCH

I'D LIKE A GLASS OF ORANGE JUICE
CERTAINLY. WHAT YEAR ?
DIK BROWNE

HAGAR'S ALWAYS WORKING... THE KIDS ARE BUSY DOING THEIR THING...
DIK BROWNE
BUT I'M STUCK IN THE HOUSE... IT REALLY GETS ME DOWN SOMETIMES
IF I DIDN'T HAVE YOU TO TALK TO I DON'T KNOW WHAT I'D DO...

HAGAR, THIS IS DOCTOR SHOOMAY
I AM GLAD TO SEE YOU

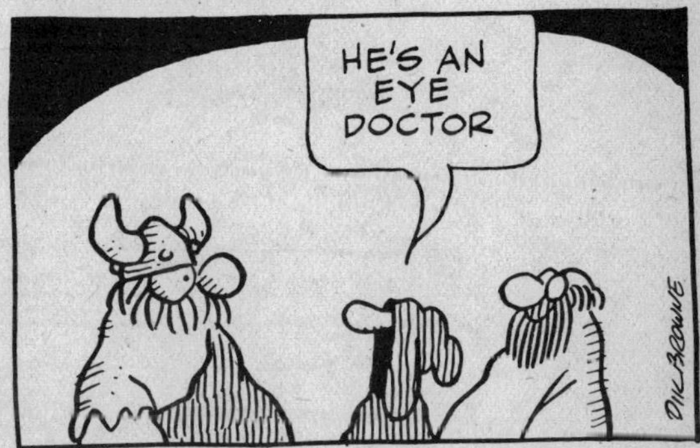
HE'S AN EYE DOCTOR
DIK BROWNE

AND MAKE IT FAST!
WISHING WELL

POOOF!
BROWNE

I WANTED A COLD BEER!
WISHING WELL

IT'S JUST A DEMON SITTING ON YOUR LIVER
BROTHER OLAF SAYS IT'S INDIGESTION

HA! THAT QUACK!
DIK BROWNE

SLAM!

YOU KNOW WHAT I HATE ?!!

LOVE!
DIK BROWNE-

DADDY SEEMS FASCINATED WITH THAT BOOK! I DIDN'T EVEN KNOW HE COULD READ!!
HE CAN'T

IT'S A COOKBOOK WITH PICTURES
DIK BROWNE

HELGA, WHILE YOU'RE UP, CAN YOU GET ME A BEER ?
ANYTHING ELSE ?!
DIK BROWNE
HOW ABOUT ONE FOR MY FRIEND ?

HEY! GIMME SOME SALT!
SALT IS BAD FOR YOU, HAGAR
DIK BROWNE

ZAP!
SEE?

IT ISN'T THAT MY CLIENT DOESN'T WANT TO PAY HIS TAXES...

HE LOVES TO PAY TAXES!!

CAREFUL! I THINK THEY'RE TRYING TO PLEAD INSANITY
DIK BROWNE

DON'T LIE TO ME! I CAN ALWAYS TELL WHEN YOU'VE BEEN DRINKING!

SHE'S SPOOKY THAT WAY...
SLAM!
DIK BROWNE

DID YOU TALK TO HAMLET ABOUT "YOU KNOW WHAT"?
NO, BUT NOT TO WORRY...

KIDS TODAY PROBABLY KNOW MORE ABOUT THE "FACTS OF LIFE" THAN I DO!

I HOPE SO
DIK BROWNE

HERE'S YOUR SCOTCH...

...AND HERE'S YOUR CHASER.
DIK BROWNE

DIK BROWNE
SIP
SIP
THE BOILING OIL IS READY, DEAR

DO YOU LIKE AGGRESSIVE WOMEN?

IF I ANSWER YOU HONESTLY, WILL YOU PROMISE NOT TO PUNCH ME OUT?
DIK BROWNE

YOU ONLY HEAR WHAT YOU WANT TO HEAR!!
YOU'RE A PERFECT BORE!
'PERFECT'? YOU REALLY THINK SO...
DIIK BROWNE

WAIT TILL YOU SEE WHAT I BROUGHT YOU FROM ITALY... A SILK DRESS... A COMB AND BRUSH... A NECKLACE... A HAIRNET...
OH, WOW!

AND 10 POUNDS OF MOZZARELLA CHEESE.

THE TAX DEPARTMENT HAS CHANGED A LOT! WE EVEN HAVE A GAME ROOM!
DIK BROWNE
WHAT GAME DO YOU PLAY?
TWENTY QUESTIONS

AS YOUR MARRIAGE COUNSELOR I SAY THAT YOUR DISAGREEMENT CAN BE SOLVED...FIRST I WANT YOU TO JOIN HANDS...

...NOW, BEST TWO OUT OF THREE WINS...
DIK BROWNE

YOU KNOW, HELGA...
I'VE BEEN THINKING...
DIK BROWNE

WHAT?!
HA HA HA HA HA HA

GUESS WHAT? A SALESGIRL JUST TOLD ME I HAD EYES LIKE BLUE STARS

SHE THOUGHT I WAS ONLY 30 YEARS OLD
WAS SHE SELLING ICE?
DIK BROWNE

YES, HOW DID YOU KNOW?

...GENTLEMEN

DID WE GET PROMOTED ?
?
DIK BROWNE

WOULD YOU EVER SELL SNERT ?
ARE YOU KIDDING? I LOVE THAT DOG!

HOW MUCH?
DIK BROWNE

IF A VIKING TELLS A LIE — HIS HORNS FALL OFF
THAT'S WHY I NEVER TELL A LIE...
BROWNE
...ER...MORE THAN I HAVE TO...
CLICK

AFTER A YEAR AT SEA I'LL BET THEY CAN'T WAIT TO SEE ME!

HOLD IT!
I JUST WAXED THE FLOOR!

REMEMBER—HAGAR IS THE HEAD OF THIS FAMILY AND IS DUE EVERY RESPECT!
DO I MAKE MYSELF CLEAR?!
DIK BROWNE

YES, MA'M!!

WHY ARE YOU HIDING?
HELGA'S IN A **WASHING** FRENZY!
BAD?
SHE'S WASHING THE DUCK!
THAT'S BAD!
DIK BROWNE

WHAT'S THE DELAY? I TOLD LUCKY EDDIE TO DROP THE DRAWBRIDGE!!
BETTER TELL HIM AGAIN

...HE GETS EVERYTHING MIXED UP
DIK BROWNE
© King Features Syndicate Inc. 1978

I WANT TWO FINGERS OF YOUR BEST BRANDY
OKAY
AND HAVE SVEN POUR IT!
THANKS, SVEN
DIK BROWNE

PERSONALLY, I THINK PEOPLE WHO USE BIG WORDS ARE PRETENTIOUS
WHAT'S 'PRETENTIOUS' MEAN ?
DIK BROWNE

WHY DO SPEAKERS USE SUCH BIG WORDS ?
JUST TRYING TO IMPRESS PEOPLE WITH THEIR BRAINS

BOY! MY FEET ARE KILLING ME!

HOW WAS AFRICA?
SANDY
DIK BROWNE

NOW STAND STILL! I'M TESTING MY SECRET TRAPDOOR
DIK BROWNE

NEEDS WORK

FOLLOW ME!!

WELL? AREN'T YOU GOING TO FOLLOW HIM?
SURE I'M GOING TO FOLLOW HIM!

AS SOON AS HE COMES UP

WHAT A WORLD!! THERE'S NOTHING YOU CAN COUNT ON!

I MEAN BESIDES FINGERS!
1...2...3...
BROWNE

WOMEN HATE TO SEE A MAN DOING NOTHING
WHY IS THAT?
BEATS ME—WHO CAN UNDERSTAND WOMEN?
DIK BROWNE

REMEMBER, THE OLD WISE MAN WILL ANSWER ONLY ONE QUESTION— SO CHOOSE CAREFULLY
IS THAT TRUE?

YES
NEXT!
DIK BROWNE

DAMES! I'M GONNA TALK TO HAGAR! HE KNOWS HOW TO HANDLE WOMEN!

HAGAR! I NEED SOME ADVICE
ABOUT WHAT?

NEVER MIND
DIK BROWNE

THE SUSPECTED SPY IS A MASTER OF DISGUISE—BUT WE THINK HE'S ONE OF THESE—
GOOD!

BUT WHICH ONE ?
DIK BROWNE

WHAT'S THAT SIGN SAY?
DIK BROWNE

BEATS ME!
STAMP OUT ILLITERACY! LEARN TO READ!

JUST THE TWO OF US ON A MOONLIT BOAT RIDE...WHAT COULD BE MORE ROMANTIC ?

MAYBE A SMALLER BOAT ??!
DIK BROWNE

RUN! IT'S RAINING!!
WHY? A LITTLE WATER IS GOOD FOR EVERYTHING!
NOT EVERYTHING!!!
DIK BROWNE

DON'T ACT INNOCENT! WHO MADE THIS MESS?!

THAT'S MORE LIKE IT! OKAY... I FORGIVE YOU.

IF WE ALL HAD TAILS LIKE YOURS THERE'D BE MORE TRUTH IN THE WORLD!
DIK BROWNE

YOU SPENT ALL MY MONEY ?!!
DON'T SHOUT!

DO YOU WANT THE WHOLE WORLD TO KNOW OUR BUSINESS ?!
DIK BROWNE

DO YOU LIKE CHESS ?
I'LL TRY ANYTHING...
DIK BROWNE
PHOOEY! TASTES AWFUL!

OH, THANK YOU, "GOTCHA!" THEY'RE BEAUTIFUL!
I'M GLAD YOU LIKE THEM, MISS HONI

I CUT THEM MYSELF
DIK BROWNE

LISTEN! I'M A HARD-WORKING GUY! I GOTTA UNWIND SOMETIME!

BEFORE BREAKFAST?!
DIK BROWNE

I HAVE A PRESENT FOR YOU
FOR ME?
YOU DARLING!
HOW DID YOU KNOW I WANTED A TOASTER?

MARRY ME AND LET ME TAKE YOU AWAY FROM ALL THIS!

DIK BROWNE
SEE! HE DOESN'T LIKE YOUR POT ROAST EITHER!

THIS IS OUR FAMOUS PUFF PASTRY
WOW!
WHY DO THEY CALL IT 'PUFF PASTRY'?
PUFF
OH...
DIK BROWNE

WANNA FIGHT ?
CROSS THIS LINE!
DIK BROWNE

IT ISN'T EXACTLY WHAT I HAD IN MIND...

NO KIDDING!
PRETTY GOOD!
I'LL SAY!

WERE YOU JUST TALKING TO YOURSELF?
I DON'T KNOW

Dik Browne
I WASN'T LISTENING

QUICKLY! QUICKLY! THERE IS A WORLD TO BE CONQUERED AND FAME TO BE WON!
OKAY! OKAY!
DIK BROWNE

I WISH YOU'D LEARN TO TIE YOUR OWN LACES!

WEREN'T YOU THE EVIL KING'S JESTER ?
YES, I USED TO DO POLITICAL SATIRE
WHAT ARE YOU DOING NOW ?
20 YEARS

FOG AHEAD!
DIK BROWNE
BONK!!
BOY! TALK ABOUT A THICK FOG!

WHEN WE WERE COURTING, YOUR FATHER CARVED OUR INITIALS IN THAT TREE
I DIDN'T KNOW DADDY COULD WRITE

HE CAN'T
DIK BROWNE

HOLD STILL AND STOP COMPLAINING!
I CAN'T HELP IT!

I *HATE* HAIRCUTS!

WHAT ARE YOU DOING ?
WASHING MY FACE

COULD THERE BE ANOTHER WOMAN ?
TIK BROWNE

THIS IS AN UNUSUAL SCOTCH
YES, IT'S A BLENDED SCOTCH

WHAT'S IT BLENDED WITH ?
CHOCOLATE MILKSHAKE
DIK BROWNE

DO ANIMALS KNOW WHAT YOU'RE THINKING?

SNERT DOES!

I AM SIR FOP. IS YOUR DAUGHTER HOME ?

HONI! THERE'S A MAN HERE WITH A STOMACHACHE!
DIK BROWNE

BOY! THE HIGHLANDS OF SCOTLAND ARE SURE RUGGED!
IT'LL BE EASIER WHEN WE GET TO THE MAIN ROAD
DIK BROWNE
THIS *IS* THE MAIN ROAD

THIS MIGHT BE ROMANTIC BUT I CAN'T SEE MY FOOD!

HOW'S THAT?

THERE'S NO PLACE LIKE HOME
DIK BROWNE

BUT WHY COMPLAIN?

IT'S A PRETTY GOOD IMITATION, BUT IT'S NOT REAL SWISS CHEESE!
HOW CAN YOU TELL?

NOTICE THE HOLES?
DIK BROWNE

DON'T EAT THOSE PEPPERS. THEY'RE TOO HOT!!
NOTHING'S TOO HOT FOR A VIKING
DIK BROWNE

HOW'S THINGS, SIR KNIGHT ?
TERRIBLE! I EVEN HAD TO SELL MY HORSE

BUSINESS THAT BAD ?
CAN'T YOU TELL ?
DIK BROWNE

BOY! DOES THAT FEEL GOOD!
DON'T LOOK AT ME LIKE THAT! MY FEET HURT! WHAT DO YOU WANT FROM ME ?!!
GET YOUR FEET OUTTA MY SOUP!

NOW WE TAKE THE VIKING OATH- 'VICTORY OR DEATH' -RAISE YOUR RIGHT HANDS!
DIK BROWNE

YOU TOO!

I DON'T KNOW WHY THEY CALL ME 'HAGAR THE HORRIBLE'

NICKNAMES ARE STUPID!
DIK BROWNE

WHY DO THEY CALL YOU 'HALF-PINT'?
SEARCH ME

WHAT'S IT LIKE LIVING WITH A BARBARIAN?

OH, IT'S OKAY
DIK BROWNE

IS THAT A MUSHROOM OR A TOADSTOOL ?

PLOP!

TOADSTOOL
DIK BROWNE

CAN YOU HAND ME ANOTHER ALE, DEAR ?
WHY DON'T YOU GET IT YOURSELF ?!
DIK BROWNE

I WOULD BUT MY HANDS ARE FULL !

TABLE FOR THREE
CERTAINLY, SIR— WILL SOMEONE BE JOINING YOU LATER ?
NO, WE'RE ALL HERE
I DON'T CARE IF IT **IS** HER BIRTHDAY—THIS IS RIDICULOUS!
KVACK!
DIK BROWNE

I HOPE WE'RE NOT KEEPING YOU FOLKS UP!
NOT AT ALL

COCK-A-DOODLE-DOO!
WE'D HAVE TO BE GETTING UP ABOUT NOW ANYWAY
DIK BROWNE

HELGA! YOUR LORD AND MASTER HAS RETURNED!!

SPLAT!

HOW ABOUT: "YOUR LOVING AND DEVOTED HUSBAND HAS RETURNED"?
DIK BROWNE

GIMME ANOTHER ONE OF THOSE
NOT TILL YOU EAT YOUR VEGETABLES!
WOMEN BARTENDERS!
DIK BROWNE

DO YOU KNOW HOW TO SHUFFLE ?
SURE
SHUFFLE
SHUFFLE
SHUFFLE
DIK BROWNE
WANT TO SEE ME DEAL ?

HAGAR! I TOLD YOU—NO FEET AND NO ELBOWS ON THE TABLE!
NOBODY TELLS ME WHAT TO DO!
DIK BROWNE

OH! YOU'RE DEFIANT!!

TODAY'S SPECIALS ARE TOMATO ASPIC SURPRISE... WATERCRESS SALAD WITH LEMON WEDGES... BABY PEAS AND CARROT SOUFFLÉ..
DIK BROWNE

OR PERHAPS YOU WOULD PREFER ONE OF OUR 'HE-MAN' ENTREES...

HELGA!
YOUR HAIR!
DIK BROWNE

OH... YOU NOTICED...

HOW MUCH?
WELL ... IT'S GOING TO BE A LONG TRIP...
DIK BROWNE

FILL 'ER UP!
XXX
XXX

NO, NO... LUCKY EDDIE GETS THE "PINK LADY" AND I GET THE "WALL BANGER"

AND WHO GETS THE RUST REMOVER ?
DIK BROWNE

I WAS BORN A VIKING!
WOW! THAT'S AMAZING
DIK BROWNE
THE HAT CAME LATER, STUPID!